a gift for

ELVERA

from

STAN

Inspired by the 1950s landmark photographic exhibition, *"The Family of Man,"* M.I.L.K. began as an epic global search to develop a collection of extraordinary and geographically diverse images portraying humanity's Moments of Intimacy, Laughter and Kinship (M.I.L.K.). This search took the form of a photographic competition — probably the biggest, and almost certainly the most ambitious of its kind ever to be conducted. With a world-record prize pool, and renowned Magnum photographer Elliott Erwitt as Chief Judge, the M.I.L.K. competition attracted 17,000 photographers from 164 countries. Three hundred winning images were chosen from the over 40,000 photographs submitted to form the basis of the M.I.L.K. Collection.

The winning photographs were first published as three books titled *Family*, *Friendship* and *Love* in early 2001, and are now featured in a range of products worldwide, in nine languages in more than 20 countries. The M.I.L.K. Collection also forms the basis of an international travelling exhibition.

The M.I.L.K. Collection portrays unforgettable images of human life, from its first fragile moments to its last. They tell us that the rich bond that exists between families and friends is universal. Representing many diverse cultures, the compelling and powerful photographs convey feelings experienced by people around the globe. Transcending borders, the M.I.L.K. imagery reaches across continents to celebrate and reveal the heart of humanity.

www.milkphotos.com

HAPPINESS

with love

M·I·L·K

MOMENTS INTIMACY LAUGHTER KINSHIP

Shared joy is double joy. Shared sorrow is half sorrow.

[SWEDISH PROVERB]

Where there is love,

there is life.

[MAHATMA GANDHI]

We wove a web in childhood, a web of sunny air.

[CHARLOTTE BRONTE]

One must ask children and birds
how **cherries** and strawberries taste.

Hold tenderly that which you cherish.

[BOB ALBERTI]

Family faces
are **magic** mirrors.

So sweet and precious is family life . . .

[JAMES MCBRIDE]

Some people move our souls to dance.

Good times made better
and bad times forgotten
due to the **healing**
magic of friendship.

[MAEVE BINCHY]

Life delights in life.

[WILLIAM BLAKE]

Seek the wisdom of the ages,

but look at the world through the eyes of a child.

[RON WILD]

Joy is not in things, it is in us.

[RICHARD WAGNER]

For memory has painted this perfect day,
with colours that never fade . . .

[CARRIE JACOBS BOND]

Grow old along with me, the best is yet to be.

Love is but the discovery of ourselves in others,
and the delight in the recognition.

[ALEXANDER SMITH]

The best and most **beautiful** things in the world cannot be seen or even touched. They must be felt with the heart.

[HELEN ADAMS KELLER]

Pages 6–7 and front cover

© Wilfred Van Zyl, South Africa

Six-year-old Marcelle holds on tight as her father, the photographer, takes her for a spin.

Page 8

© Surendra Pradhan, India

Amid the paddy fields of rural India, the faces of two young workers are illuminated by laughter and friendship.

Pages 10–11

© Peter Gabriel, USA

A fashion-conscious trio discover the perfect accessory as they sit in a café in New York.

Pages 12–13

© Marcy Appelbaum, USA

In Jacksonville, Florida, USA, two-year-old Rachel is curious to see if her belly button matches her father's.

Page 15

© Michael Chiabaudo, USA

As his friends stride out along a dusty village street near Tijuana, Mexico, a young boy – and his trousers – try to keep up.

Page 16

© Lori Carr, USA

Body paint and childhood imagination bond young warriors Billy and Shaun in San Rafael, California, USA.

Page 17

© Amit Bar, The Netherlands

A comfortable sofa is the ideal spot for three-year-olds Allon and Tom to share laughter and play. The young friends live at the Kfar Hamaccabi Kibbutz in Israel.

Pages 18–19

© Lynn Goldsmith, USA

A little girl holds tightly to her grandmother's hand as they walk together in Arles, France.

Page 20

© George Peirce, USA

Puppy love in Point Pleasant, New Jersey, USA. Twelve-year-old DD and her sister Georgia, 10, are delighted with their new pet. Their photographer father, George Peirce, captured this moment as they met eight-week-old Atlantis for the very first time.

Page 21

© Jacqueline Parker, UK

The best of friends – inseparable childhood companions Christopher, aged seven, and his dog Billy take a break from making mischief.

Pages 22–23

© Shannon Eckstein, Canada

Rubbing noses in Vancouver, Canada – new father Davy finds the perfect way to bond with his baby daughter, Ciara, only nine days old.

Page 24

© Noelle Tan, USA

Bonnie's enthusiastic greeting is matched by a delighted smile from friend Nancy in Washington DC, USA.

Page 25

© Roberto Colacioppo, Italy

A great-grandmother's heartfelt embrace of a young bride. The old lady, 97, and her great-granddaughter are the only family members who still live in the mountain village of Roccaspinalveti, Italy.

Pages 26–27

© Stefano Azario, UK

Like mother, like daughter – at a New York airport, there's still time for nine-month-old Verity and her mother, Lydzia, to play before the long flight home to England.

Page 28

© Darien Mejía-Olivares, USA

Dancing partners – as two-year-old toddlers Harry and Margaret take to the floor in New York, USA, they can't resist giving each other a hug.

Page 31

© Bill Frantz, USA

Music to the ears – budding saxophonist Sarah, aged two, entertains her baby sister, Leslie, in Wisconsin, USA.

Page 32

© Eddee Daniel, USA

A moment of discovery in Sauk City, Wisconsin, USA, as one-year-old Chelsea realises where the music is coming from.

Page 33
© Shauna Angel Blue, USA
Chicago, Illinois, USA – dressed in her favourite tutu, two-year-old Rose dances to the tune of her mother's harp.

Pages 34–35
© Christopher Smith, USA
Age is no barrier to enjoying a dance at a wedding party in North Carolina, USA. New bride, Pamela, teaches Uncle Mac the steps, while the bride's parents show how it should be done.

Pages 36–37
© Jinjun Mao, China
In Shuinan village, China, the mischievous antics of a five-year-old visitor amuse and delight his grandfather and friends.

Page 39
© Dharmesh Bhavsar, Canada
Free wheeling – a rolling wheel leads an energetic race for three companions on a deserted road in Baroda, India.

Page 40
© Shannon Eckstein, Canada
The rain has stopped in Chilliwack, British Columbia, Canada, and 18-month-old Kiana can't wait to explore a new puddle with the help of her puppies, Tasia and Belle.

Page 41
© David M Grossman, USA
Brother and sister – six-year-old Ethan gives four-year-old Emory an enthusiastic hug at a birthday party in Brooklyn, New York.

Pages 42–43
© Thanh Long, Vietnam
The faces of six young friends as they take a break from lessons at their school in Phan Rang city, Vietnam.

Pages 44–45
© Rinaldo Morelli, Brazil
Me and my shadow – during a visit to the zoo, young Brazilians Pietro, aged four, and Yuri, five, are inspired to create their own weird and wonderful animals.

Pages 46–47
© John Kaplan, USA
Double happiness – as Xia Yongqing, 84, and his nephew Yang Ziyun, 82, share a joke in the village of Nanyang in the Sichuan province of China.

Page 48
© Malie Rich-Griffith, USA
Laughter is infectious for two friends from Mgahinga village, Uganda.

Page 50
© Neil Selkirk, USA
Open wide – on a trip to the beach in Wellfleet, Massachusetts, USA, nothing interests Zane more than her mother, Susan.

Page 51
© Thomas Patrick Kiernan, Ireland
A young boy shares his delight with his mother as he paddles in the water on Coney Island, New York.

Page 52
© K Hatt, USA
Free fall – four bikini-clad friends leap off a pier into the water below in Miami, Florida, USA.

Page 54
© Sam Tanner, UK
Laughter and a loving embrace for a Jewish couple celebrating 61 years of marriage. Dave, 89, and his wife, Renee, 82, live in the East End of London, England.

Page 56
© Paul Knight, New Zealand
In the small, bustling town of Wajima in Japan, a local resident is eager to pass on the latest news to her friend.

Page 57
© Deborah Roundtree, USA
The surprise party – a grandmother delights in the company of her grandchildren as she celebrates her 85th birthday in Yakima, Washington, USA.

Page 59
© Nicholas Ross, UK
Smiling through – on a dusty pavement in the slums of Bombay, India, friendship blossoms for 12-year-old Indou and her blind companion, Mala.

Back cover
© Cristina Piza, Germany
Musicians and old friends Ruben and Ibrahin celebrate the release of their new CD at a café in Madrid, Spain.

First published by Helen Exley Giftbooks in 2003,
16 Chalk Hill, Watford, Herts, WD19 4BG, UK.

First published by Helen Exley Giftbooks LLC in 2004,
185 Main Street, Spencer, MA 01562, USA.

6 8 10 12 11 9 7

ISBN 978 1 86187 603 4

Designed by Kylie Nicholls. Printed in China.
Back cover quotation by Richard Wagner.

M·I·L·K™

MOMENTS INTIMACY LAUGHTER KINSHIP